# Taste of the Lowcountry

charleston
cooks!
maverick kitchen store

&

Danielle Wecksler

**GIBBS SMITH**
TO ENRICH AND INSPIRE HUMANKIND

Salt Lake City | Charleston | Santa Fe | Santa Barbara

First Edition
15  14  13            10  9  8

Text © 2007 Charleston Cooks! and Danielle Wecksler

Published by
Gibbs Smith
P.O. Box 667
Layton, Utah 84041

Orders: 1-800.835.4993
www.gibbs-smith.com

Designed by Gibbs Smith
Printed and bound by Artistic Printing, Salt Lake City, Utah

Library of Congress Cataloging-in-Publication Data
Taste of the lowcountry / Charleston cooks and Danielle Wecksler. — 1st ed.
    p. cm.
 Includes bibliographical references and index.
 ISBN-13: 978-1-4236-0199-9 (alk. paper),   ISBN-10: 1-4236-0199-8 (alk. paper)
 1. Cookery, American—Southern style. 2. Cookery—South Carolina. I. Wecksler, Danielle.
 TX715.2.S68T373 2007
 641.5'9757—dc22                                    2006030886

*This book is dedicated to the maverick
minds who envisioned the fun, unique culinary
center that ultimately became Charleston Cooks!,
and to the thousands of home cooks who have
joined us in the kitchen for good food,
laughter, education, and fun.*

# Contents

**Introduction** 6

**Appetizers**
Buttermilk Biscuits 10
Bread and Butter Pickles 12
Corn Fritters 13
Fried Green Tomatoes 14
Fried Oysters 15
Pickled Shrimp Salad 16
Sweet and Spicy Pecans 18

**Salads and Soups**
Lowcountry Okra Soup 20
Shrimp Stock 22
Mixed Greens with Pecans, Blue Cheese,
    and Shoestring Sweet Potatoes 24

Summer Tomato Soup 25
Warm Green Bean and Tomato Salad 26
Watermelon Arugula Salad 28

**Main Dishes**
BBQ Pork 32
Crab Cakes 33
Crispy Chicken with Pan Gravy 34
Fish Croquettes 36
Grilled Pork Tenderloin with Bourbon
    Bacon Sauce 38
Lowcountry Gumbo 40
Pecan-Encrusted Grouper 42
Shrimp and Grits 43

**Sauces, Rubs, and Relishes**
  Basic Brine 46
  Benne Seed Caramel Sauce 47
  Dry Rub 48
  Sweet Mustard BBQ Sauce 49
  Sweet Pepper Relish 50
  Tartar Sauce 51
  Warm Bacon Vinaigrette 52

**Sides**
  Blue Cheese Cole Slaw 54
  Broccoli Cheese Casserole 56
  Butter Bean Mash 58
  Braised Cabbage 60
  Carolina Rice and Vegetable Saute 61
  Cheddar Scallion Grit Cakes 62
  Clemson Blue Cheese and Grits Souffle 64
  Country Ham and Cornbread Stuffing 66

  Cowpea Succotash 68
  Horseradish Sweet Potatoes 70
  Hoppin' John 71
  Red Rice 72
  Sweet Potato and Date Hash 74

**Desserts**
  Apple Pecan Cobbler 76
  Banana Pudding 78
  Carolina Gold Rice Pudding 80
  Grilled Peaches with Pound Cake 81
  Chocolate Peanut Butter "Pie" 82
  Grandma's Pecan Pie 84
  Sweet Potato Strawberry Shortcakes 86
  Blueberry Lime Parfaits 88

**Index** 90

# Introduction

*Taste of the Lowcountry* is a must-have book for the best in lowcountry cuisine. This cookbook is a collection of recipes from Taste of the Lowcountry cooking classes held at the Charleston Cooks! Maverick kitchen store in Charleston, South Carolina. The recipes feature the secrets behind this popular regional culinary draw and are perfect for anyone who wants to prepare those favorite dishes at home.

Since its inception in 2004, Charleston Cooks! has become a favorite stop for those who are passionate about cuisine. This kitchen store, part of the

Maverick Southern Kitchens culinary group, has everything from high-performance kitchen tools and appliances to gifts, cookbooks and culinary gadgets. In its state-of-the-art demonstration kitchen, cooking classes from top area chefs are offered on a variety of topics, skills, and menus. With *Taste of the Lowcountry* cookbook, every home chef can prepare the cuisine that is the cornerstone of the coastal South Carolina heritage.

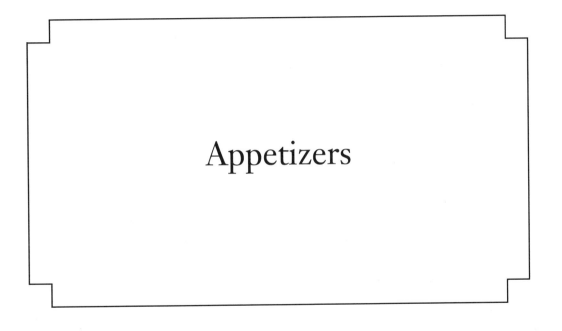

Appetizers

# Buttermilk Biscuits

### Makes about 2 dozen biscuits

2 cups flour
2 teaspoons baking powder
½ teaspoon baking soda
¼ teaspoon salt

1 tablespoon sugar
6 ounces cold unsalted butter, cut in ½-inch chunks
¼ cup buttermilk

1. Preheat oven to 350 degrees. Combine flour, baking powder, baking soda, salt, and sugar in a large bowl.
2. Cut in butter using a pastry cutter or two knives until mixture resembles coarse meal. Add buttermilk and stir just to combine into a soft dough.
3. Gather dough into a ball and place on floured surface. Using floured hands, knead dough 3 to 5 times. Roll out dough to about ½ inch thickness. Cut out rounds of desired size. Place biscuits on a parchment-lined baking sheet very close to each other and to the sides of the pan.
4. Bake for about 10 to 15 minutes, or until light golden brown.

Variations:
## Country Ham and Cheese

*2  slices country ham, diced*
*¼  cup grated cheddar cheese*

## Blue Cheese and Pecan

*½  cup blue cheese crumbles*
*½  cup chopped pecans*

## Sweet Potato

*1  sweet potato, peeled and grated*

Add additional ingredients to the flour mixture along with the buttermilk, and then proceed with the rest of the recipe.

# Bread and Butter Pickles

## Makes about 1 quart pickles

2½ cups sugar
½ cup cider vinegar
2 tablespoons mustard seed
1 tablespoon celery seed
1 quart cucumbers, sliced

¼ cup kosher salt
1 yellow bell pepper, sliced in strips
1 red bell pepper, sliced in strips
1 onion, sliced
1 clove garlic

1. Place sugar, vinegar, mustard and celery seeds in a large saucepan and heat over low heat until sugar dissolves. Remove from heat and let mixture cool.
2. Place cucumbers in a strainer or colander and toss with salt. Let sit for 10 minutes to allow them to "weep." Rinse cucumbers well and then pat dry.
3. Place cucumbers, bell peppers, onion, and garlic in a large airtight container. Pour sugar mixture over the vegetables. Store in the refrigerator for at least one week before using.

**Tip:** Pickles keep well in the refrigerator for up to one month.

# Corn Fritters

## Serves 6 to 8

3 ears corn, shucked
1 egg
½ cup milk
⅓ cup stone-ground grits
2 tablespoons baking powder

2 to 3 tablespoons flour
2 to 3 green onions, sliced
Canola oil
Salt

1. Cut corn off the cob and then scrape the cob with back of knife to extract the corn milk.
2. Place egg and milk in a mixing bowl and whisk together until combined. Add the grits, baking powder and flour and then stir in the corn, corn milk, and green onions.
3. Pour oil in a nonstick pan just to cover the bottom and heat over medium heat until hot. Drop batter into hot skillet by the tablespoon. Fry on both sides until golden brown. Remove from pan and pat off excess oil on paper towels. Lightly sprinkle salt over fritters.

**Tip:** The batter will be thin and runny, but will firm up when dropped onto the hot skillet.

# Fried Green Tomatoes

## Serves 8

*Canola oil*
*1 cup flour*
*Salt and pepper*
*4 eggs*
*¼ cup milk*

*1 cup breadcrumbs*
*1 cup cornmeal*
*3 tablespoons blackening seasoning*
*3 large green tomatoes, firm but ripe, sliced*
*¼ inch thick*

1. Pour 2 inches of canola oil in a large, heavy saucepan; preheat oil to 350 degrees.
2. Place flour in a shallow dish and season with salt and pepper.
3. Place eggs and milk in another shallow dish and whisk together.
4. Place breadcrumbs and cornmeal in a third dish and mix with blackening seasoning.
5. Dredge tomatoes in flour and shake off excess, dip in the egg mixture and allow any excess egg to drip off, and then dredge in the breadcrumb mixture until well coated.
6. Place tomatoes in hot canola oil and fry in batches until golden brown on both sides.
7. Drain fried tomatoes on paper towels and lightly sprinkle with salt.

**Tip:** The tomatoes go well with the Sweet Pepper Relish on page 50.

# Fried Oysters

## Serves 8

Canola oil
1   pound shucked oysters in oyster juice
2   cups yellow cornmeal

2   tablespoons blackening seasoning
Salt

1. Pour 2 inches of canola oil in a large saucepan and preheat oil to 350 degrees.
2. Drain oysters in a strainer or colander; discard the liquid.
3. Place cornmeal and blackening seasoning in a shallow dish and mix well together.
4. Dredge oysters in cornmeal mixture until coated well.
5. Place coated oysters in the hot oil and fry in batches until golden brown and crisp.
6. Drain fried oysters on paper towels and sprinkle lightly with salt.

**Tip:** Fried oysters go well with the Sweet Pepper Relish on page 50 or the Tartar Sauce on page 51.

# Pickled Shrimp Salad

## Serves 8

8 to 10 small green beans, ends trimmed and
   cut in half
1 pound shrimp, peeled and deveined
½ cup white wine vinegar
2 to 3 shallots, diced
1 tablespoon minced garlic
1 tablespoon sugar
2 tablespoons lemon juice
1 tablespoon celery seed

1 tablespoon crushed red pepper flakes
¼ cup finely chopped fresh dill
¼ cup capers
1 to 2 tablespoons caper juice
½ cup olive oil
6 to 8 canned artichoke hearts, roughly chopped
½ red onion, thinly sliced
Salt and pepper

1. Fill a medium stockpot two-thirds full with water and place on high heat. Salt water heavily and bring to a gentle boil.
2. Fill a large bowl with half water and half ice to make an ice bath.
3. Gently drop green beans into the boiling water and cook for 30 seconds. Remove the green beans from the water using a skimmer and then submerge in the ice bath.

4. Gently drop shrimp into the boiling water and cook until slightly pink. Remove shrimp from the water using a skimmer and then submerge in the ice bath. Remove green beans and shrimp from the ice bath and pat dry.
5. Place vinegar, shallots, garlic, sugar, lemon juice, celery seed, red pepper flakes, dill, capers, and caper juice in a large mixing bowl and whisk together. Add the olive oil to the mixture, a little at a time, whisking constantly until well combined.
6. Fold the shrimp, green beans, artichoke hearts, and onion into the vinegar mixture. Season to taste with salt and pepper.

**Tip:** Shrimp will continue to "cook" in the vinegar mixture, so this dish should be served immediately. If not serving immediately, follow recipe as noted except leave out the shrimp until ready to serve.

# Sweet and Spicy Pecans

### Makes about 1 cup nuts

½ cup sugar
1 cup pecan halves
Large pinch of salt

Pinch of cayenne pepper
1 tablespoon unsalted butter

1. Place sugar in a medium saute pan and melt over low heat until light golden brown, stirring occasionally.
2. Stir in the nuts, salt, cayenne pepper, and butter; stir to coat the nuts well with the sugar mixture.
3. Spread nuts out on a baking sheet and let cool. When cool, break apart into chunks.

**Tip:** You can substitute walnuts, pistachios, hazelnuts, cashews, or just about any other kind of nut for the pecans.

# Soups and Salads

# Lowcountry Okra Soup

### Serves 8

2 smoked ham hocks
1 quart water
2 tablespoons unsalted butter
1 onion, diced
1 tablespoon minced garlic
2 carrots, diced
2 stalks celery, diced
1 16-ounce can chopped tomatoes, with juice
1 red or yellow bell pepper, diced

2 tablespoons fresh thyme, leaves picked off the stems and chopped
2 bay leaves
15 to 20 okra, sliced
2 to 3 ears corn, shucked and kernels cut off the cob
2 tablespoons sugar
2 to 3 dashes hot sauce
Salt and pepper

1. Place ham hocks and water in a large stockpot. Bring water to a boil and boil ham hocks until meat starts to fall off the bone, about 1 hour.
2. Strain off liquid and reserve; this will be your pork stock. Slightly chill ham hocks and pick off the meat. Save meat, but discard fat and bones.
3. Place butter in a large stockpot and melt over medium-high heat. Add the onion to

the pot and saute until translucent. Stir in the garlic, carrots, and celery and cook for about 2 minutes.
4. Add the reserved pork stock, tomatoes with juice, bell pepper, thyme, and bay leaves. Bring to a simmer and cook for 5 minutes.
5. Add the okra and corn to the pot and bring to a simmer. Add the reserved ham hock meat and season to taste with sugar, hot sauce, salt, and pepper.

## Variation:
## Charleston Clam Chowder

6  *strips bacon, diced*
1  *quart chicken stock*
2  *russet potatoes, peeled and diced*
1  *pound clams, roughly chopped*

Use bacon in place of the ham hocks and the chicken stock in place of the pork stock. Add potatoes to the stockpot along with the tomatoes, and add the clams to the pot along with the okra.

# Shrimp Stock

Makes about 2 quarts stock

2 tablespoons unsalted butter
Shells from 1 to 2 pounds of shrimp
2 tablespoons tomato paste
1 clove garlic, smashed
1 stalk celery, chopped
1 to 2 carrots, chopped
1 medium onion, chopped
2 sprigs parsley

3 bay leaves
2 sprigs thyme
1 star anise
3 whole cloves
5 whole coriander seeds
7 whole black peppercorns
½ cup white wine
About 1½ to 2 quarts water

1. Place butter in a medium stockpot over medium-high heat. When melted, add the shrimp shells and cook until pink and just starting to turn golden brown.
2. Add tomato paste, garlic, celery, carrots, onion, parsley, bay leaves, thyme, star anise, cloves, coriander seeds, and peppercorns to the pot and continue to cook for about 2 to 3 minutes.
3. Add the white wine to the pot (mixture will boil up vigorously) and cook until the

wine is reduced to an almost syrupy consistency, about 5 to 10 minutes.
4. Add enough water to the pot to barely cover the shells and bring to a simmer. Simmer for 30 to 45 minutes and then strain through a fine strainer. Discard the shells, vegetables, and herbs and reserve the stock.

## Variation:
## Shrimp Bisque

½   *cup bourbon*
2   *quarts heavy cream*

Substitute bourbon for the white wine and use heavy cream in place of the water. Increase the cooking time to about 2 hours and then strain and serve with a whole cooked shrimp as a garnish.

# Mixed Greens with Pecans, Blue Cheese, and Shoestring Sweet Potatoes

### Serves 6 to 8

Canola oil
1 sweet potato, sliced in very thin strips
using a mandoline
Salt
1 14-ounce bag prewashed mixed greens

Salad dressing of choice
½ pint grape tomatoes, halved lengthwise
¼ cup pecans, toasted and roughly chopped
¼ cup blue cheese crumbles

1. Pour about 1 inch of canola oil in a large saute pan and heat oil to about 350 degrees.
2. Place sweet potato strips in the hot oil and fry in batches until light brown. Remove from the oil and drain on paper towels. Sprinkle lightly with salt.
3. Place a small bunch of mixed greens neatly mounded on each plate and drizzle a small amount of desired dressing over top.
4. Arrange tomatoes, pecans, and blue cheese over greens. Top with fried sweet potatoes.

**Tip:** The Warm Bacon Vinaigrette on page 52 is very good with this salad.

# Summer Tomato Soup

## Serves 6 to 8

2 to 3 seedless cucumbers, peeled and finely
    chopped
¼ cup basil, chiffonade
6 to 8 red or yellow tomatoes, peeled and seeded
1  white onion, roughly chopped
1  red bell pepper, roughly chopped
1  tablespoon garlic, roughly chopped

¼ cup sherry wine vinegar
¼ cup olive oil plus more for garnish
2  tablespoons cumin
½ cup seasoned croutons
1  tablespoon sugar
1  teaspoon hot sauce
Salt and pepper

1. Set aside some of the cucumber and all of the basil for garnish.
2. Place all other ingredients into a food processor and pulse until fairly smooth, but still a little chunky. Season to taste with salt and pepper.
3. Place soup in a well chilled bowl and garnish with reserved cucumber, basil, and a drizzle of olive oil.

**Tip:** To chiffonade basil, stack 2 to 3 leaves basil on top of each other, roll like a cigar and then, using a sharp knife, cut across the rolled basil to make thin ribbons.

# Warm Green Bean and Tomato Salad

## Serves 6 to 8

Water
Salt
1 to 2 large tomatoes
½ pound green beans, ends trimmed
1 tablespoon unsalted butter
¼ cup canola oil
1 onion, diced

¼ cup toasted walnuts
½ cup sherry vinegar
½ pint grape tomatoes, halved lengthwise
1 tablespoon minced garlic
1 tablespoon sugar
3 tablespoons basil, chiffonade
Pepper

1. Fill a large stockpot two-thirds full with water and place on high heat. Salt the water heavily and bring to a boil.
2. Fill a large bowl with half water and half ice to make an ice bath.
3. Score bottoms of tomatoes with an X. Place tomatoes in boiling water for 10 to 15 seconds. Pull the tomatoes out of the water and place in the ice bath. As soon as the tomatoes are cool enough to handle, remove from ice bath and peel off the skin. Cut tomatoes in half horizontally and squeeze out the seeds. Roughly chop the tomatoes.

4. Place the green beans into the boiling water until they turn bright green, about 45 seconds. Pull the green beans out of the water and place in the ice bath; drain.
5. Place the butter and oil in a large saute pan and melt over medium heat. Add the onion to the pan and cook until translucent.
6. Add the green beans, walnuts, vinegar, chopped tomatoes, grape tomatoes, garlic, and sugar to the pan and cook for 1 to 2 minutes more.
7. Add the basil to the pan and then immediately turn off the heat. Season to taste with salt and pepper.

## Variation:
## Warm Okra and Tomato Salad

*½ pound okra, sliced*

Substitute okra for the green beans and omit step 4.

# Watermelon Arugula Salad

## Serves 6 to 8

1 *shallot, minced*
¼ *cup fig balsamic vinegar*
¼ *cup canola or olive oil*
1 *tablespoon fresh thyme, leaves picked off the stems and chopped*
*Salt and pepper*

1 *14-ounce bag prewashed baby arugula*
2 *cups watermelon (preferably yellow), rind cut off and flesh cut into 1-inch cubes*
¼ *cup toasted pistachios*
⅓ *cup crumbled ricotta salata or feta cheese*

1. Place shallot and vinegar in a small bowl and let sit for 10 minutes. Whisk in oil and thyme and season to taste with salt and pepper.
2. Place the arugula in a large bowl and drizzle some of the dressing on top, tossing lightly to coat. Place some of the arugula mounded on each plate.
3. Top the arugula with the watermelon, pistachios, and ricotta salata or feta.

**Tip:** You may not need to use all of the dressing. The greens should be lightly coated with the dressing, but not drowning in it. Leftover dressing can be kept in the refrigerator for up to 2 weeks and can be used on any salad.

Variation:
## Grilled Peach Arugula Salad

*16 thin slices country ham*
*4  firm ripe peaches, pitted and cut in quarters*
*Canola oil*

Preheat grill on high until hot and then reduce heat to medium. Wrap a slice of ham around each peach quarter. Brush grill with canola oil and place peaches on grill. Grill, turning occasionally, until ham is crisp and peaches are softened. Remove from grill, and substitute peaches for the watermelon in the above recipe.

# Main Dishes

# BBQ Pork

## Serves 6 to 8

Canola oil
2  pounds pork shoulder
1  carrot, diced
1  onion, diced

1  stalk celery, diced
1/4  cup red wine
1/2  cup pork or chicken stock

1. Preheat oven to 250 degrees. Heat a large oven-proof saute pan until hot. Add some canola oil to just cover the bottom of the pan and allow to get hot. Add the pork shoulder and sear pork until browned on all sides. Remove from pan and set aside.
2. In the same pan, add the carrot, onion, and celery and saute for 1 minute. Add wine and cook another minute. Add stock to the pan and bring to a simmer.
3. Add the pork shoulder back into the pan and then cover with a tight-fitting lid. Place pan in preheated oven for 2 to 3 hours, or until the meat is tender and falling apart. Remove meat from pan, and discard vegetables. When meat is cool enough to handle, pull apart with fingers.

**Tip:** Toss the BBQ pork with the Sweet Mustard BBQ Sauce on page 49 before serving.

# Crab Cakes

## Serves 6 to 8

4 tablespoons mayonnaise
½ red bell pepper, finely diced
4 scallions, thinly sliced
1 teaspoon dry mustard
5 tablespoons breadcrumbs

2 teaspoons lemon juice
Dash of hot sauce
1 pound lump crabmeat, picked over for
   shells and cartilage
Canola oil

1. Place mayonnaise, bell pepper, scallions, mustard, breadcrumbs, lemon juice, and hot sauce in a large mixing bowl; mix well. Gently fold in crabmeat and toss together. Season to taste with salt and pepper. Place crab mixture in the refrigerator for 15 minutes.
2. Remove crab mixture from the refrigerator and form crab cakes into balls of desired size.
3. Pour enough canola oil in a medium saute pan to cover bottom and then heat until hot. Fry crab cakes in oil until browned on both sides and warmed through.

**Tip:** Good crab cakes should taste like crab—not breadcrumbs. If the crab cake balls are not holding their shape, add a little more breadcrumbs to the mixture a few tablespoonfuls at a time.

# Crispy Chicken with Pan Gravy

## Serves 6

6  chicken breasts
2  cups flour plus more for gravy
Salt and pepper
2  eggs

2  tablespoons milk
Canola oil
½  cup chicken stock
Splash of heavy cream

1. Rinse chicken and pat dry. Pound chicken between sheets of plastic wrap until uniform in thickness.
2. Place 2 cups flour in a shallow dish and season to taste with salt and pepper.
3. Place eggs and milk in another shallow dish and whisk until combined.
4. Dredge a piece of chicken in the flour mixture and shake off excess flour. Dip floured chicken into the egg mixture to coat and allow any excess to drip off. Dredge chicken back into the flour mixture. Repeat with each piece of chicken.
5. Pour about 1 inch of canola oil in a heavy skillet (enough oil to come about halfway up the chicken pieces) and heat to about 350 degrees. Add chicken to the hot oil, and fry in batches until golden brown and internal temperature is 160 degrees.

6. Remove chicken from the pan and drain on paper towels. Drain all but ¼ cup of the oil and fat remaining in the skillet.
7. Sprinkle enough flour into the skillet to make a paste that is the consistency of wet sand. Whisk flour into oil and cook flour until it smells nutty. Add the chicken stock and whisk constantly over medium heat until sauce is thickened and smooth. Add more chicken stock if sauce is too thick. Add a splash of heavy cream to the gravy and season to taste with salt and pepper.

**Tip:** When seasoning the gravy, use a lot more fresh cracked pepper than you normally would—it tastes great!

# Fish Croquettes

## Serves 4 to 6

1   pound fish scraps (such as grouper, flounder, or salmon), ground
1   medium onion, diced
1   clove garlic, minced
¼   cup capers, chopped
1   tablespoon lemon juice
½   cup sour cream
¼   cup breadcrumbs plus more for breading

2   tablespoons fresh dill, leaves picked off the stems and chopped
2   tablespoons fresh parsley, leaves picked off the stems and chopped
1   egg
Dash of hot sauce
Salt and pepper
Canola oil

1. Place ground fish, onion, garlic, capers, lemon juice, sour cream, ¼ cup breadcrumbs, dill, parsley, egg, and hot sauce in a large mixing bowl and mix well. Season with salt and pepper.
2. Place some breadcrumbs into a shallow dish. Form the fish mixture into patties of desired size, and then dredge in breadcrumbs.

3. Heat about 1 inch of canola oil in a large saute pan over medium heat until hot. Add fish patties and cook on both sides until golden brown and cooked through.
4. Remove croquettes from the oil and pat off excess oil with paper towels.

**Tip:** The croquettes go well with the Tartar Sauce on page 51.

# Grilled Pork Tenderloin with Bourbon Bacon Sauce

### Serves 4 to 6

| | |
|---|---|
| 1 whole pork tenderloin, trimmed of silver skin and excess fat | 6 slices bacon, diced |
| Salt and pepper | ½ medium red onion, diced |
| Canola oil | 1 cup bourbon |
| | 1 cup reduced brown stock |

1. Preheat oven to 350 degrees. Season pork tenderloin all over with salt and pepper.
2. Heat a heavy oven-safe saute pan over medium-high heat until it smokes. Add a little canola oil just to coat the bottom of the pan and then add the pork tenderloin. Sear pork tenderloin on all sides until golden brown.
3. Place the pan in the oven, and cook pork tenderloin until medium-rare (about 145 degrees internal temperature). Remove the pan from the oven and transfer the pork tenderloin to a cutting board; let rest while making the sauce.
4. Place bacon in a medium saute pan and cook over medium heat until golden brown

and crispy. Add the onion to the pan and cook until translucent.

5. Remove the pan from the heat and add the bourbon. Scrape up any brown bits from the bottom of the pan and return pan to the heat. Add the stock to the pan and cook until it is reduced slightly and thickened. Season to taste with salt and pepper.

**Tip:** Add bacon to a cold saute pan, since this will allow more of the fat to melt into the pan. If bacon is added to a pan that is already hot, it will sear in the pan and not as much fat will come out of the bacon.

# Lowcountry Gumbo

## Serves 8

1   pound shrimp, peeled and deveined
    *(shrimp shells reserved)*
2   cups chicken stock
4   tablespoons unsalted butter
1   onion, diced
1   tablespoon minced garlic
2   stalks celery, diced
1   green bell pepper, diced
1   red or yellow bell pepper, diced
2   tablespoons flour
1   tablespoon seafood boil seasoning
1   16-ounce can chopped tomatoes with juice

¼   pound andouille sausage, sliced in rounds
2   tablespoons fresh thyme leaves, leaves
    picked off the stems and chopped
2   bay leaves
2   tablespoons sugar
8 to 10 okra, sliced in rounds
1   ear corn, shucked and kernels cut off cob
3   dashes hot sauce
2   teaspoons Worcestershire sauce
Salt and pepper
2   cups cooked rice
1   bunch scallions, thinly sliced

1. Heat a medium saucepan over medium-high heat. Add the shrimp shells to the pan and cook until the shells are pink and starting to turn brown. Add the chicken stock to the pan, and simmer for 30 minutes; strain and reserve the liquid and discard the shrimp shells. This will be your shrimp stock.
2. Place the butter in a large stockpot and melt over medium heat. Add the onion to the pot, and cook until translucent. Add the garlic and celery to the pot and cook for 1 minute. Add the peppers and cook for another minute. Add the flour and seafood boil seasoning to the pot and cook for 2 to 3 minutes more.
3. Add the reserved shrimp stock, tomatoes with juice, sausage, thyme, bay leaves, and sugar to the pot and bring to a simmer; cook for about 7 minutes.
4. Add the okra, corn, and shrimp to the pot. Cook just until shrimp turn pink and are barely cooked through.
5. Add the hot sauce and Worcestershire and then season to taste with salt and pepper. To serve, place a scoop of the cooked rice in each bowl and top with a scoop of the gumbo. Garnish with the chopped scallions.

**Tip:** For the seafood boil seasoning, you can use Charleston Cooks! Lowcountry Seafood Boil, Old Bay, or any other similar seasoning.

# Pecan-Encrusted Grouper

## Serves 6

1   cup shelled pecans
2   tablespoons flour
1½ pounds grouper fillets

*Salt and pepper*
*Canola oil*

1. Place the pecans in the bowl of a food processor and finely grind. Place in a shallow dish and mix with the flour.
2. Season grouper all over with salt and pepper. Dredge grouper in the pecan mixture, ensuring that the grouper is covered all over with coating.
3. Heat a large heavy saute pan over high heat. Add enough canola oil to cover the bottom of the pan.
4. Add the grouper to the pan and cook until light golden brown on both sides and fish is cooked through—about 2 to 3 minutes on each side, depending on thickness of fillets.

**Tip:** Fish is cooked through when it looks opaque, is firm and springy to the touch, and you can see tiny globes of white on the edges of the fish. Any firm white fish can be used in this recipe, as well as any kind of nut.

# Shrimp and Grits

## Serves 6

2 to 3 slices bacon, diced
½ onion, chopped
1 clove garlic, minced
2 teaspoons blackening seasoning
1 pound shrimp, deveined and shelled
  (reserve shells for Shrimp Stock)

1 ear corn, shucked and kernels cut off cob
6 to 8 okra, sliced in rounds
8 to 12 grape tomatoes, halved
1 recipe Shrimp Stock (see page 22)
2 tablespoons unsalted butter
Salt and pepper

1. Place bacon in a large saute pan and cook over medium heat until light golden brown and crispy. Add the onion to the pan and cook until translucent. Add the garlic and blackening seasoning and saute in the bacon fat until fragrant. Add the shrimp and allow them to sit in the pan untouched for 1 minute; do not stir.
2. Add the corn, okra, and tomatoes to the pan and stir to incorporate. Add enough stock to cover shrimp about halfway. Bring to a boil and reduce sauce slightly, about 5 minutes. Turn off the heat and fold in the butter. Season to taste with salt and pepper.

**Tip:** Shrimp stock should be served over Cheddar Scallion Grit Cakes on page 62.

# Sauces, Rubs, and Relishes

# Basic Brine

## Makes about ½ gallon brine

½ gallon water
⅓ cup kosher salt
2 tablespoons sugar
3 cloves garlic, crushed
Pinch of red pepper flakes

5 whole cloves
2 star anise
1 teaspoon whole black peppercorns
3 bay leaves
2 sprigs fresh thyme

1. Place all ingredients in a soup pot and bring to a boil. Reduce heat and simmer until salt is dissolved; remove brine from the heat and chill completely.
2. Add uncooked meat to the cold brine and allow to soak completely submerged in brine overnight or about 8 hours (but not more than 24 hours).
3. Remove meat from brine and rinse very quickly with cool water. Pat dry with paper towels and prepare meat as usual.

**Tip:** The brine will add moisture and flavor to leaner cuts of meat like chicken or pork loin.

# Benne Seed Caramel Sauce

### Makes about 1 cup sauce

¼ *cup cream*
½ *cup sugar*
1 tablespoon unsalted butter

*Pinch of salt*
¼ *cup benne seeds (sesame seeds)*

1. Place cream in a small saucepan over low heat until warm. Keep warm while making caramel.
2. Place sugar in a heavy saute pan and melt over low heat until light golden brown, stirring occasionally.
3. Remove sugar mixture from heat and whisk in the warm cream. Caution, as mixture will bubble up vigorously. Keep whisking until caramel is smooth again. Whisk in butter and salt, and then fold in benne seeds.

**Tip:** Do not toast the benne seeds before adding them to the caramel. The caramel is so hot that they will burn when added to the caramel if they are already toasted. This sauce can be drizzled over any dessert, but is especially good with the Carolina Gold Rice Pudding on page 80.

# Dry Rub

Makes about ¾ cup rub

3 tablespoons smoked paprika
2 tablespoons brown sugar
1 tablespoon dry mustard
1 tablespoon garlic powder
1 tablespoon onion powder
1 tablespoon dried basil
½ tablespoon ground bay leaves

½ tablespoon salt
½ tablespoon ground coriander
½ tablespoon dried thyme
½ tablespoon black pepper
½ tablespoon white pepper
½ tablespoon cumin

1. Mix all ingredients together in a mixing bowl and store in a cool, dry place.

**Tip:** Rub can be used for beef, pork, chicken, or any other type of poultry. Generally, rub should be applied a day before cooking to allow flavors to develop. Then meat can be roasted, seared, grilled, or smoked.

# Sweet Mustard BBQ Sauce

## Makes about 2 cups sauce

¼  *cup finely diced onion*
1  *clove garlic, minced*
½  *cup cider vinegar*
¼  *cup ketchup*
1  *cup yellow mustard*
1  *tablespoon Worcestershire sauce*

2 to 3 *dashes hot sauce*
¼  *cup water*
6  *ounces cola (½ of a 12 ounce can)*
1  *ear corn, shucked and kernels removed*
   *from cob*

1. Place onion, garlic, and vinegar in a medium saucepan. Cook over medium heat until the vinegar is reduced and syrupy, about 10 to 15 minutes.
2. Add the remaining ingredients to the pan and bring to a simmer until slightly thickened, about 20 minutes. Season to taste with salt and pepper.

**Tip:** This sauce goes well with chicken, pork, or BBQ beef.

# Sweet Pepper Relish

### Makes about 2 cups relish

1  *yellow bell pepper, diced*
1  *red bell pepper, diced*
1  *red onion, diced*
1  *jalapeño pepper, seeded and finely chopped*
1  *tablespoon minced garlic*

1  *cup sugar*
¾  *cup cider vinegar*
1  *tablespoon grated fresh ginger*

1. Combine all ingredients in a large stockpot and bring to a simmer. Cook until thickened and reduced by about one-third, stirring frequently, about 45 minutes.

**Tip:** Relish will last several months in the refrigerator in an airtight container and is an excellent accompaniment for fish, pork, or chicken.

# Tartar Sauce

### Makes about 1 cup sauce

½ cup mayonnaise
1 tablespoon apricot-jalapeño jelly or Sweet Pepper Relish (see page 50)
1 to 2 teaspoons hot sauce
2 tablespoons capers, roughly chopped

3 tablespoons fresh tarragon, finely chopped
½ small onion, finely diced
1 teaspoon minced garlic
½ tablespoon lemon juice
Salt and pepper

1. Whisk together all ingredients in a small bowl. Season to taste with salt and pepper.

**Tip:** Be sure to taste the sauce before serving and add more salt, pepper, hot sauce, or lemon juice if desired. This sauce is good with almost any seafood dish!

# Warm Bacon Vinaigrette

### Makes about 1 cup vinaigrette

3 slices thick-cut bacon, diced
1 large shallot, diced
1 clove garlic, minced
1 teaspoon fresh thyme, leaves picked off the
  stems and chopped

1 teaspoon lemon juice
¼ cup sherry wine vinegar
Salt and pepper

1. Place bacon in a small saute pan. Cook over medium heat until golden brown and crispy.
2. Pour bacon and fat into a mixing bowl and whisk in all other ingredients. Season to taste with salt and pepper.

**Tip:** This vinaigrette needs to be served warm or the bacon fat will start to harden. If this happens, just place the bowl over very low heat to melt the fat again.

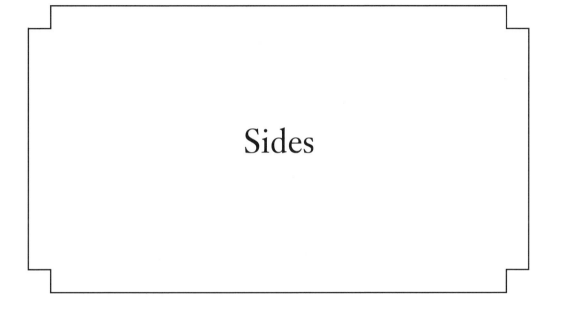

Sides

# Blue Cheese Slaw

## Serves 6 to 8

2 to 3 carrots, peeled
½ large or 1 small head cabbage, thinly sliced
1 bunch scallions, thinly sliced
1 egg
3 tablespoons rice wine vinegar
1 tablespoon lemon juice

1 tablespoon Dijon mustard
Dash of hot sauce
1 cup canola oil
Salt and pepper
1 cup blue cheese crumbles

1. Shred carrot on the large holes of a box grater.
2. Place carrots, cabbage, and scallions in a large mixing bowl and set aside.
3. Place egg, vinegar, lemon juice, Dijon mustard, and hot sauce in a blender or food processor. Pulse for a few seconds to combine the ingredients and then, with blender still running, slowly drizzle the canola oil into the blender container until the mixture becomes thick and creamy like mayonnaise. Season to taste with salt and pepper.

4. Pour some of the mayonnaise mixture over the vegetables and toss together to lightly coat. Add the blue cheese crumbles and gently toss again.

**Tip:** The mayonnaise is also called an "aioli." Any left over from this recipe can be kept in a covered container in the refrigerator for about a week and substituted in any recipe calling for mayonnaise.

# Broccoli Cheese Casserole

## Serves 8

2 tablespoons unsalted butter, plus more for
   buttering dish
1½ cups broccoli florets, cut in 1-inch pieces
4 eggs
2 egg yolks

2 cups heavy cream
1 cup grated cheddar cheese
Dash of freshly grated nutmeg
   Salt and pepper

1. Preheat oven to 350 degrees. Butter a 9 x 13-inch baking dish and set aside.
2. Fill a large bowl with half water and half ice to make an ice bath.
3. Bring a large stockpot filled two-thirds full with water to a boil. Add broccoli and cook for about 3 to 5 minutes, or until broccoli is bright green and slightly softened. Remove broccoli from the water and submerge immediately in the ice bath.
4. Remove broccoli from the ice bath and place in a saute pan. Cook over low heat until broccoli is dry.

5. Place the eggs, egg yolks, and cream in a large mixing bowl and whisk well to combine. Stir in the broccoli and cheese. Season with the nutmeg, salt, and pepper.
6. Pour mixture into the buttered baking dish and bake for approximately 1 hour, or until casserole is firm and set.

**Tip:** You can substitute other cooked vegetables for the broccoli, such as yellow squash, cauliflower, spinach, butternut squash, etc.

# Butter Bean Mash

## Serves 6

2   medium potatoes, peeled and cut in large
    chunks
2   cups fresh or frozen butter beans
½   cup unsalted butter, divided

½   onion, diced
1   cup chicken stock
¼ to ½ cup milk

1. Fill a large saucepan two-thirds full with water, add potatoes, and bring to a boil; cook potatoes until soft. Drain the potatoes and place in a large mixing bowl.
2. While potatoes cook, fill a small saucepan two-thirds full with water, add butter beans, and bring water to a boil; cook beans until slightly softened. Drain the beans and set aside.
3. In a small saucepan, melt 2 tablespoons butter over medium heat. Add the onion and saute until translucent.
4. Add half of the cooked butter beans and the chicken stock to the pan; cook until beans are tender, but not falling apart, and the stock is slightly reduced.

5. Add the onion mixture to the bowl with the potatoes and mash with a potato masher until creamy.
6. Stir in the milk, remaining butter, and butter beans. Thin with additional milk if mash is too thick. Season to taste with salt and pepper.

**Tip:** Lima beans will also work in this recipe but may need to be cooked longer, because they are generally not as tender as butter beans.

# Braised Cabbage

## Serves 8

3  slices bacon, diced
1  onion, thinly sliced
1  head purple cabbage, sliced
1  cup champagne vinegar

¼  cup brown sugar
1  Granny Smith apple, cored and thinly
   sliced
Salt and pepper

1. Place bacon in a large saute pan and cook over medium-high heat until golden brown and crispy. Add the onion to the pan and cook until translucent.
2. Add the cabbage to the pan and saute for 1 to 2 minutes, or just until cabbage becomes slightly limp.
3. Add the vinegar and brown sugar to the pan and then scrape up any brown bits from the bottom.
4. Continue cooking over low heat until the cabbage is slightly softened.
5. Add the apples and cook until they are slightly softened. Remove from heat and season to taste with salt and pepper.

**Tip:** Other vinegars work well in this recipe too. Try sherry, balsamic, or white wine vinegar.

# Carolina Rice and Vegetable Saute

## Serves 6 to 8

1 carrot, peeled
4 tablespoons unsalted butter, divided
½ onion, diced
1 cup fresh corn kernels
8 to 10 okra, sliced into rounds
1 zucchini, diced

½ cup chicken stock
½ pint grape tomatoes, halved lengthwise
2 cups cooked rice
¼ cup basil, chiffonade
Salt and pepper

1. Shred the carrot on large holes of a box grater and set aside. Heat a saute pan over medium-high heat. Melt 2 tablespoons butter in the pan and then add onion; cook until translucent. Add the corn, okra, zucchini, and carrot; cook for 1 to 2 minutes.
2. Add the chicken stock and bring to a simmer. Cook the vegetables in the stock until they are just tender, about 3 to 5 minutes.
3. Fold in the tomatoes and rice; cook 1 minute more. Remove pan from heat and stir in the remaining butter and basil. Season to taste with salt and pepper.

**Tip:** Any vegetables in season can be used in this recipe.

# Cheddar Scallion Grit Cakes

## Serves 8

3   cups water
½   teaspoon salt
2   tablespoons unsalted butter, divided
1   cup stone-ground grits
1   cup heavy cream
1   cup grated cheddar cheese

1   small bunch scallions, thinly sliced
Dash of hot sauce
Salt and pepper
Cornmeal
Canola oil

1. Place water, salt, and 1 tablespoon butter in a medium saucepan; bring water to a boil.
2. Add the grits to the boiling water, stir well, and reduce heat to low. Cook grits over low heat, stirring occasionally until they are thick and creamy, about 40 minutes. Mix in the cream and remaining butter.
3. Remove the pan from the heat and stir in the cheddar cheese and scallions. Add the hot sauce and season to taste with salt and pepper.
4. Pour the grits into a shallow sheet pan and spread in an even layer. Place pan in the refrigerator until grits are cool and hardened.

5. Remove pan from the refrigerator and cut the grits into round cakes of desired size using a biscuit cutter.
6. Place some cornmeal in a shallow dish. Dredge grit cakes in cornmeal and coat well on both sides.
7. Pour about 1/8 inch canola oil into a large saute pan and heat over medium-high heat until hot.
8. Carefully place grit cakes in hot oil and fry until golden brown on both sides.

**Tip:** Grits can also be served immediately after adding the cheese and scallions, simply mounded on a plate.

# Clemson Blue Cheese and Grits Souffle

## Serves 4

⅛ cup grits
⅜ cup water
2 tablespoons unsalted butter, plus more for
  buttering dish
¼ cup milk

½ cup crumbled Clemson blue cheese
¼ cup grated Parmesan cheese
3 egg whites
1 tablespoon cream of tartar

1. Place grits, water, and butter in a medium saucepan, stir well, and bring to a simmer. Cook grits until they are creamy, about 30 minutes, stirring occasionally.
2. Remove pan from the stove and stir in the milk. Allow grits to cool to room temperature. Mix in the blue cheese once the grits are cool.
3. Preheat oven to 350 degrees.
4. Generously butter a 4-cup souffle dish. Sprinkle Parmesan cheese on bottom and sides of dish and then tap out any excess.
5. Whip the egg whites with the cream of tartar in a stand mixer until stiff peaks hold.

6. Very gently fold the egg whites into the grits until well combined. Carefully pour mixture into buttered souffle dish and bake for 30 to 40 minutes, or until springy to the touch and light golden brown on top.

**Tip:** Souffles need to be served immediately, because they start to fall as soon as they are removed from the oven.

# Country Ham and Cornbread Stuffing

## Serves 6 to 8

2  tablespoons unsalted butter, plus more for
   casserole dish
½  cup thinly sliced country ham
1  onion, diced
1  tablespoon minced garlic
2  cups crumbled cornbread

1  tablespoon fresh thyme, leaves picked off
   the stems and chopped
1  cup fresh corn kernels
½  cup chicken stock
1  egg, lightly beaten
Salt and pepper

1. Preheat oven to 350 degrees. Generously butter a 9 x 13-inch casserole dish.
2. Heat a large saute pan over medium heat. Add the butter and ham and cook until ham is starting to turn brown around the edges.
3. Add the onion to the pan and saute until translucent. Add the garlic and cook until fragrant. Add the cornbread to the pan and mix well.
4. Transfer the ham mixture to a large bowl, mix in the thyme, corn, chicken stock, and egg, and season to taste with salt and pepper.

5. Pour the stuffing into the buttered casserole dish and bake for about 30 minutes, or until the top is light golden brown.

**Tip:** This stuffing can also be used to stuff chicken breasts, game hens, turkey, pork chops, or pork loin.

# Cowpea Succotash

## Serves 6 to 8

2   cups cowpeas
Water
4   slices bacon, diced
½   onion, diced
1   tablespoon minced garlic
1   ear corn, shucked and kernels removed
    from cob

8 to 10 okra, sliced in rounds
1   cup chicken stock
½   pint grape tomatoes, halved lengthwise
3   tablespoons basil, chiffonade
2   tablespoons unsalted butter
Salt and pepper

1. Place cowpeas in a small saucepan and cover with cold water. Bring water to a simmer and cook until cowpeas are tender.
2. Place bacon in a large saute pan and cook over medium heat until bacon is brown and crispy. Add onion to the pan and cook until translucent.
3. Add the garlic to the pan and cook until fragrant.
4. Add the cooked cowpeas, corn, okra, and chicken stock to the pan and bring to a simmer. Cook for a few minutes until stock is slightly reduced.

5. Add tomatoes and basil to the pan and cook for 1 minute.
6. Turn off the heat and stir in the butter. Season to taste with salt and pepper.

**Tip:** This dish can also be made with butter beans, lima beans, black-eyed peas, or any other field pea.

# Horseradish Sweet Potatoes

## Serves 4 to 6

2 *large sweet potatoes, peeled and cut in large chunks*
¼ *cup cream*
1 *stick unsalted butter*

8 *ounces prepared horseradish*
1 *tablespoon honey*
*Salt and pepper*

1. Preheat oven to 350 degrees. Fill a large stockpot two-thirds full with water and bring to a boil. Add potatoes and cook until easily pierced with a fork.
2. Drain the potatoes and place them on a baking sheet. Place the pan in the oven, occasionally turning the potatoes, for about 10 to 15 minutes, or until potatoes are dry and fluffy.
3. Remove potatoes from the oven and, while still hot, quickly push through a food mill or ricer and into a large bowl.
4. Mix in the cream, butter, horseradish, and honey. Season to taste with salt and pepper.

**Tip:** Add more horseradish if you want the potatoes to be spicier, more honey if you want them sweeter, and more cream or butter if you want them creamier.

# Hoppin' John

## Serves 6 to 8

4 cups water
1 cup cowpeas
1 bay leaf
2 to 3 slices thick-cut bacon, diced
½ onion, diced

1 cup uncooked rice
2 cups pork stock
Dash of hot sauce
Salt and pepper

1. Place water, cowpeas, and bay leaf in a small saucepan. Bring water to a simmer and cook cowpeas until they are tender but not mushy; strain and set aside.
2. Place bacon in a saucepan and cook over medium heat until golden brown and crispy. Add the onion and cook until translucent. Add the rice and stir well to coat with bacon fat.
3. Add the pork stock to the pan and bring to a boil. Reduce the heat, cover, and simmer until the rice is cooked and liquid is absorbed, about 15 minutes.
4. Fold the cowpeas into the rice, add the hot sauce, and season to taste with salt and pepper.

**Tip:** An easy way to make homemade pork stock is to boil a 1 to 2 ham hocks in about 1 quart of water for about 1 hour. Skim off any fat and store stock in the refrigerator.

# Red Rice

## Serves 8

Canola oil
1   red onion, diced
1   green bell pepper, diced
2   cups uncooked rice
3   tablespoons blackening seasoning or
    Cajun seasoning
1   tablespoon minced garlic

3½ cups water
1   tablespoon sugar
1   tablespoon tomato paste
½   cup tomato juice
2   bay leaves
1   bunch scallions, thinly sliced
Salt and pepper

1. Heat a saucepan over medium heat. Add enough canola oil to cover the bottom of the pan.
2. When the oil is hot, add the onion to the pan and cook until translucent. Add the bell pepper, uncooked rice, and blackening seasoning to the pan and then saute until rice and seasoning is fragrant, about 2 to 3 minutes.
3. Add the garlic to the pan and saute until fragrant, about 1 minute.
4. Add the water, sugar, tomato paste, tomato juice, and bay leaves to the pan and stir until paste is incorporated.

5. Bring mixture to a simmer and cook, covered, until rice is cooked and liquid has been absorbed, about 15 to 20 minutes.
6. Stir in the scallions and season to taste with salt and pepper.

**Tip:** Don't forget to remove bay leaves from the rice before serving.

# Sweet Potato and Date Hash

Serves 4 to 6

4  slices bacon, diced
1  red onion, thinly sliced
2  sweet potatoes, peeled and diced
About ½ cup chicken stock
½  cup green beans, cut in ½-inch segments

½  cup chopped dried dates
½  cup chopped pecans
1  tablespoon fresh thyme, leaves picked off
   the stems and chopped
Salt and pepper

1. Place bacon in a large saute pan, and cook over medium heat until golden brown and crispy. Add the onion to the pan and cook until light golden brown.
2. Add the potatoes to the pan and enough chicken stock to come halfway up the potatoes. Cook until potatoes are softened and stock has reduced by about half.
3. Add the green beans to the pan and cook for just a few minutes until they have softened just a bit but are still crunchy.
4. Stir in the dates, pecans, and thyme. Season to taste with salt and pepper.

**Tip:** Any other kind of potato or root vegetable can be used in this recipe. Or, the type of nut or herb can also be varied, according to your tastes.

# Desserts

# Apple Pecan Cobbler

## Serves 8

3  Granny Smith apples, cored and cut in
   ½-inch cubes
3  tablespoons bourbon
2  tablespoons brown sugar
1  stick unsalted butter, softened
1  cup sugar
1  egg

1  cup flour
1  teaspoon baking powder
1  teaspoon cinnamon
Pinch of salt
½  cup sour cream
½  cup pecan pieces

1. Preheat oven to 350 degrees. Place the apples, bourbon, and brown sugar in a small mixing bowl. Toss together and let sit while making cobbler topping.
2. Place the butter and sugar in the bowl of a stand mixer and beat together until light and fluffy. Add the egg to the bowl and mix briefly. Add the flour, baking powder, cinnamon, and salt. Mix to combine all ingredients.
3. Add the sour cream and pecans to the bowl and stir by hand just until incorporated.

4. Place apples in bottom of a 9 x 13-inch baking dish and then drop the topping by the spoonful over them. Do not spread topping. Bake in preheated oven until topping is golden brown and firm on top, about 35 to 40 minutes.

## Variations:
### Peach Cobbler
3   *tablespoons peach liqueur*
3 to 4 *ripe peaches, sliced*

### Berry Cobbler
3   *tablespoons berry liqueur*
1   *cup mixed fresh berries (like strawberries, blueberries, raspberries)*

### Pear Walnut Cobbler
3   *tablespoons bourbon*
3 to 4 *ripe pears, sliced*
½   *cup walnut pieces*

Substitute the liqueur, fruit, or nuts with any of these combinations.

# Banana Pudding

## Serves 8

½ cup granulated sugar
⅓ cup flour
Dash of salt
4 egg yolks
2 cups milk

2 tablespoons banana liqueur or extract
2 cups angel food cake or pound cake, cut in
   1-inch cubes
1 cup bourbon or rum
5 to 6 ripe bananas, sliced

1. Place sugar, flour, and salt in the top part of a double boiler. Whisk in the egg yolks and milk.
2. Place water in the bottom of the double boiler. Bring water to a gentle boil over medium heat. Cook the flour and egg mixture over the water until thickened and the consistency of pudding. Remove pudding from heat and let cool slightly.
3. Stir the banana liqueur or extract into the pudding.
4. Spread a small amount of the pudding in the bottom of a deep 9-inch square dish. Top with a layer of the cubed cake. Drizzle some of the bourbon over the cake and

top with a layer of sliced bananas. Pour about one-third of the remaining pudding over the bananas.

5. Continue layering cake, bourbon, bananas, and pudding, ending with a layer of pudding. Top with a few slices of banana for garnish.

**Tip:** In order to avoid scorching the pudding, keep the heat on low while constantly whisking. Also remember that the pudding will continue to set up after you remove it from the heat, so remove it a little earlier than the desired consistency.

# Carolina Gold Rice Pudding

## Serves 8

2  *cups cream*
2  *cups milk*
1  *cup uncooked Carolina Gold rice*

½  *cup sugar*
1  *tablespoon vanilla extract*
1  *orange, zested and juiced*

1. Place cream, milk, rice, and sugar in a large saucepan and stir well to combine. Bring mixture to a gentle simmer and cook until rice is tender and creamy and most of the liquid is absorbed, about 30 minutes.
2. Remove pan from heat and stir in the vanilla extract, and orange zest and juice.
3. Place rice pudding in the refrigerator and chill well before serving.

**Tip:** Leftover rice pudding can be made into fritters. Simply roll cold rice pudding into balls, coat with cornmeal, and fry in canola oil until golden brown all over. Serve with the Benne Seed Caramel Sauce on page 47.

# Grilled Peaches with Pound Cake

## Serves 8

4  *firm ripe peaches, halved and pitted*
*Canola oil*
4  *slices pound cake, cut in half*

4  *tablespoons unsalted butter*
½  *cup brown sugar*

1. Heat grill on high until hot. Brush peach halves with a little oil and grill until charred and slightly softened. Remove from grill and let cool slightly. Cut peaches into chunks.
2. Grill pound cake slices until lightly toasted on both sides. Remove from grill and set aside.
3. Place butter and brown sugar in a saute pan and stir over low heat until butter is melted. Add the peach chunks to the pan, and cook until the brown sugar is melted and the sauce is slightly thickened and coats the peaches.
4. To serve, top the pound cake slices with some of the peaches and juices from the pan.

**Tip:** Pears, nectarines, plums, and apricots can be grilled and served the same way as the peaches.

# Chocolate Peanut Butter "Pie"

## Serves 8 to 10

4   tablespoons unsalted butter, plus more for
    buttering pan
3   ounces bittersweet chocolate, roughly chopped
Pinch of salt
½   cup brown sugar
2   eggs
1   teaspoon vanilla extract

⅓   cup flour
1   cup powdered sugar
1   cup peanut butter
1   8-ounce package cream cheese, softened
1   cup heavy cream
Chocolate syrup

1. Preheat oven to 350 degrees. Generously butter an 9-inch pie dish.
2. Place butter and chocolate in a medium saucepan and cook over low heat until melted.
   Remove from heat and let cool slightly.
3. Whisk the salt and brown sugar into the chocolate mixture. Next, whisk in the eggs
   and vanilla extract, and continue whisking until batter is smooth. Add the flour and
   whisk just until incorporated.
4. Pour the batter into the buttered pie dish. Bake until toothpick inserted in the cen-

ter of the cake comes out clean, about 20 minutes. Let cool to room temperature.

5. While cake is baking, make peanut butter filling. Place powdered sugar, peanut butter, and cream cheese in the bowl of a food processor and blend together until smooth.

6. Whip cream until soft peaks hold, and then very gently fold the peanut butter mixture into the whipped cream.

7. Top cooled cake with peanut butter mixture. Smooth top and then drizzle with chocolate syrup. Place "pie" in the refrigerator for at least an hour to firm up.

**Tip:** Do not use chunky or natural peanut butter for this recipe, as it will not work as well.

# Grandma's Pecan Pie

## Serves 8

1 cup sugar
½ cup light corn syrup
½ cup dark corn syrup
3 eggs, slightly beaten
2 tablespoons unsalted butter, melted

1 teaspoon vanilla
3 tablespoons bourbon
1 cup chopped pecans
1 pie crust, "blind baked" and cooled to room temperature (see Tip)

1. Preheat oven to 425 degrees.
2. Place sugar, corn syrups, eggs, butter, vanilla, and bourbon in a mixing bowl and stir to combine well.
3. Sprinkle pecans onto bottom of pie crust and then pour the sugar mixture over top.
4. Place pie in the oven and bake for 10 minutes. Then reduce heat to 350 degrees and cook for about 30 to 40 minutes more, or until golden brown on top and firm (not runny) in the center. If the pie crust browns too quickly, cover the edges with foil to prevent it from burning.

5. Cool completely before cutting.

**Tip:** To blind bake a pie crust, line the crust with foil or parchment paper. Place pie weights or dried beans on top and bake the crust at 350 degrees until just barely pale

# Sweet Potato Strawberry Shortcakes

## Serves 8

2   pints strawberries, sliced
⅓   cup sugar
1   orange, zested
¼   cup balsamic vinegar
¼   cup mint, chiffonade
2   cups flour
2   teaspoons baking powder

½   teaspoon salt
2½ tablespoons sugar, plus more for sprinkling
     on tops
1½ cups heavy cream, plus more for brushing
     on tops, divided
1   large sweet potato, finely grated

1. Preheat oven to 425 degrees. Place strawberries, sugar, orange zest, vinegar, and mint in a small mixing bowl and stir to combine. Set aside while making shortcakes.
2. Sift the flour, baking powder, salt, and sugar into a large mixing bowl.
3. Add 1 cup cream and the grated potato to the bowl. Stir just to combine into a soft dough. Gather dough into a ball and place on a floured surface. Using floured hands, gently knead about 4 to 5 times.
4. Roll out dough on a floured surface to about ½ inch thickness. Cut out rounds of desired

size. Place shortcakes on a parchment-lined baking sheet, spaced about 1 inch apart. Brush tops with additional cream and sprinkle with additional sugar.

5. Bake shortcakes until light golden brown, about 15 to 20 minutes. Remove from oven and let cool slightly.

6. While shortcakes are baking, whip the remaining ½ cup cream until soft peaks form.

7. To serve, cut a warm shortcake in half horizontally. Place the bottom half of the short cake on a plate, and top with a spoonful of the berries and berry liquid, a spoonful of whipped cream, and the top of the shortcake.

## Variation:

Shortcakes can also be made savory. Reduce the amount of sugar to 1 tablespoon, and substitute 1 cup grated cheddar or crumbled blue cheese for the sweet potato.

# Blueberry Lime Parfaits

## Serves 8

3 tablespoons unsalted butter
3 tablespoons sugar
½ cup graham cracker crumbs
2 pints blueberries
½ cup raspberry liqueur
¼ cup sugar

1 8-ounce container mascarpone cheese,
  softened
¼ cup fresh lime juice
¼ cup heavy cream
2 tablespoons sugar
2 limes, zested

1. Place butter in a small saucepan and melt over low heat. Mix in 3 tablespoons sugar and graham cracker crumbs. Continue to cook over low heat until crumbs are golden brown. Remove from heat and set aside to cool.
2. Place the blueberries, liqueur, and ¼ cup sugar in a mixing bowl; set aside.
3. Whisk together the mascarpone cheese, lime juice, cream, and 2 tablespoons sugar in another mixing bowl. Continue whisking until soft peaks form.
4. Place a dollop of the cheese mixture in a parfait glass.

5. Top with a sprinkle of the crumb mixture, and a scoop of the blueberries (with the juice).
6. Repeat the three layers, ending with the cheese mixture. Top with lime zest.

**Tip:** If you are unable to find mascarpone cheese, you can substitute cream cheese.

# Index

aioli, 55
andouille sausage, 40
angel food cake, 78, 79
Appetizers, 9–18
apple, 60, 76, 77
Apple Pecan Cobbler, 76
apricot, 81
artichoke hearts, 16, 17

baby arugula, 28
bacon, 21, 38, 52, 60, 68, 71
banana, 78, 79
banana liqueur, 78
Banana Pudding, 78
Basic Brine, 46

BBQ Pork, 32
beef, 48, 49
bell peppers: green, 40, 72; yellow, 12, 20, 21, 40, 50; red, 12, 20, 21, 25, 33, 40, 50
Benne Seed Caramel Sauce, 47
benne seeds, 47
Berry Cobbler, 77
berry liqueur, 77
biscuits: Blue Cheese and Pecan Biscuits, 11; Buttermilk Biscuits, 10; Country Ham and Cheese Biscuits, 11; Sweet Potato Biscuits, 11
blackening seasoning, 14, 15, 43, 72
black-eyed peas, 69

Blue Cheese Coleslaw, 54
Blueberry Lime Parfaits, 88
blueberries, 77, 88, 89
bourbon, 23, 38, 39, 76, 77, 78, 79, 84
Braised Cabbage, 60
Bread and Butter Pickles, 12
brine, 46
broccoli, 56, 57
Broccoli Cheese Casserole, 56
Butter Bean Mash, 58
butter beans, 58, 59, 69
buttermilk, 10
Buttermilk Biscuits, 10
butternut squash, 57

cabbage, 54, 60
Cajun seasoning, 72
capers, 16, 17, 36, 51

caramel sauce, 47
Carolina Gold rice, 80
Carolina Gold Rice Pudding, 80
Carolina Rice and Vegetable Saute, 61
carrots, 20, 21, 22, 32, 54, 61
cauliflower, 57
celery, 20, 21, 22, 32, 40, 41
Charleston Clam Chowder, 21
Cheddar Scallion Grit Cakes, 62
cheese: cheddar, 11, 56, 57, 62, 87;
    blue, 11, 24, 54, 55, 64, 87;
    Parmesan, 64; ricotta salata, 28;
    feta, 28; cream, 82, 83, 89;
    mascarpone, 88, 89
chicken, 34, 35, 46, 48, 49, 50, 67
chocolate, bittersweet, 82
Chocolate Peanut Butter "Pie," 82
chocolate syrup, 82, 83

clams, 21
Clemson blue cheese, 64
Clemson Blue Cheese and Grits Souffle, 64
cobbler, 76, 77
cola, 49
coleslaw, 54
Corn Fritters, 13
corn, 13, 20, 21, 40, 41, 43, 49, 61, 66, 68
cornbread, 66
Country Ham and Cornbread Stuffing, 66
cowpeas, 68, 71
Cowpea Succotash, 68
Crab Cakes, 33
crabmeat, 33
cream, 23, 34, 35, 47, 56, 62, 70, 80, 82, 86, 87, 88
Crispy Chicken with Pan Gravy, 34
croquettes, 36, 37

crust, pie, 84, 85
cucumbers, 12

dates, dried, 74
Desserts, 75–89
Dry Rub, 48

fish, 36, 37, 42, 50
Fish Croquettes, 36
flounder, 36
Fried Green Tomatoes, 14
Fried Oysters, 15
fritters, 13, 80

game hens, 67
ginger, 50
graham cracker crumbs, 88
Grandma's Pecan Pie, 84

Granny Smith apple, 60
gravy, 34, 35
green beans, 16, 17, 26, 27, 74
Grilled Peach Arugula Salad, 29
Grilled Peaches with Pound Cake, 81
Grilled Pork Tenderloin with Bourbon
    Bacon Sauce, 38
grits, 13, 62, 63, 64, 65
grouper, 36, 42
gumbo, 41

ham, 11, 29, 66
ham hocks, 20, 21, 71
Hoppin' John, 71
horseradish, 70
Horseradish Sweet Potatoes, 70
hot sauce, 20, 21, 25, 33, 36, 40, 41, 49,
    51, 54, 62, 71

jalapeño, 50
jalapeño jelly, apricot-, 51

lima beans, 59, 69
limes, 88
Lowcountry Gumbo, 40
Lowcountry Okra Soup, 20

Main Dishes, 31–43
mixed greens, 24
Mixed Greens with Pecans, Blue Cheese,
    and Shoestring Sweet Potatoes, 24

nectarine, 81
nuts: pecans, 11, 18, 24, 42, 74, 76, 84;
    hazelnuts, 18; cashews, 18; pistachios,
    18, 28; walnuts, 18, 26, 27, 77

okra, 20, 21, 27, 40, 41, 43, 61, 68
orange, 80, 86
oysters, 15

peach, 29, 77, 81
Peach Cobbler, 77
peach liqueur, 77
peanut butter, 82, 83
pear, 77, 81
Pear Walnut Cobbler, 77
Pecan-Encrusted Grouper, 42
Pickled Shrimp Salad, 16
pickles, 12
pie crust, 84, 85
plums, 81
pork shoulder, 32
pork tenderloin, 38, 46, 48, 49, 50, 67
potatoes: russet, 21, 58, 59; sweet potato,

11, 24, 70, 74, 86, 87
pound cake, 78, 81
pudding, 78, 79

raspberry, 77
raspberry liqueur, 88
Red Rice, 72
relish, 14, 15
rice, 40, 41, 61, 71, 72, 73, 80
rub, dry 48
rum, 78

salmon, 36
Sauces, Rubs, and Relishes, 45–52
sausage, 40, 41
seafood boil seasoning, 40, 41
sesame seeds, 47
shortcake, 86, 87

shrimp, 16, 17, 22, 40, 41, 43
Shrimp and Grits, 43
Shrimp Bisque, 23
Shrimp Stock, 22
Sides, 53–74
souffle, 64, 65
Soups and Salads, 19–29
spinach, 57
stocks: brown, 38; chicken, 21, 32, 34, 35, 40, 58, 61, 66, 68, 74; pork, 21, 32, 71
stuffing, 66, 67
strawberries, 77, 86
Summer Tomato Soup, 25
Sweet and Spicy Pecans, 18
Sweet Mustard BBQ Sauce, 49
Sweet Pepper Relish, 50
Sweet Potato and Date Hash, 74

Sweet Potato Strawberry Shortcakes, 86
Tartar Sauce, 51
tomatoes: green, 14; canned, 20, 21, 40, 41; grape, 24, 26, 27, 43, 61, 68, 69; soup, 25; red, 25, 26, 27; yellow, 25

Warm Bacon Vinaigrette, 52, 24
Warm Green Bean and Tomato Salad, 26
Warm Okra and Tomato Salad, 27
watermelon, 28, 29
Watermelon Arugula Salad, 28
wine: red, 32; white, 22, 23

yellow squash, 57

zucchini, 61

# About the Author

Danielle Wecksler became a culinary professional after spending years in management positions with Silicon Valley IT companies. Her love of cuisine drew her to attend prestigious cooking schools in Italy and San Francisco, after which she instructed cooking classes at Sur La Tables before moving to the East Coast. As General Manager and Culinary Instructor for Charleston Cooks!, Danielle shares her passion for cuisine with home chefs from around the country. She resides in Charleston with her husband, Andrew.